Broken on Purpose

by

Pastor Alan L. Chester

Trilogy Christian Publishers

A Wholly Owned Subsidary of Trinity Broadcasting Network

2442 Michelle Drive

Tustin, CA 92780

For information, address Trilogy Christian Publishing

Rights Department, 2442 Michelle Drive, Tustin, Ca 92780.

Trilogy Christian Publishing/ TBN and colophon are trademarks of Trinity Broadcasting Network.

For information about special discounts for bulk purchases, please contact Trilogy Christian Publishing.

Manufactured in the United States of America

10 9 8 7 6 5 4 3 2 1

Library of Congress Cataloging-in-Publication Data is available.

B-ISBN#: 978-1-64773-532-6

E-ISBN#: 978-1-64773-533-3

Dedication

This book is dedicated to my wife, Dr. Shanta L. Chester. Thank you for inspiring me to begin writing again. Your love and patience have renewed my hope and faith in the greatness of God within me.

To all our children, Kosha, Kisha, Michael, Thomas, David, Daniel, Darius, Alan Jr. Christopher, and Caleb. To all of our grandchildren, Jabar, Janiah, Amielia, Lyondon, Kay Kay, Brooklyn, Micheal, Mandy, Jacob, Kendell, Jo Jo, David, Shane, Reese; our daughter-in-laws Kate, Brianna, Mini, and Amanda; and our godchildren Khloe and Virick. I love you all with all of my heart.

To my mother, Doris Chester, and father, Lewis Gettings, thank you for introducing me to the name of Jesus. I miss you so much. To my sister, Dr. Sylvia James, thank you for believing in me when I didn't even believe in myself.

To my brother, Steven Chester, thank you for always being there.

To my father and mother-in-law, Elder Joseph and Sister Rosetta Stevens, thank you for your great love and support.

Finally to my Fresh Fire Ministries Church Family and my Assistant Pastor Elder Daron Stewart, thank you for your continued love and support. I am honored to be your Pastor.

Contents

Preface

One of my favorite household chores is washing dishes. Many may find it to be a troublesome task, but I enjoy it immensely. For me, there is nothing like the poignant scent of dishwashing liquid, the invitingness of the warm sudsy water, and the sound of squeaky clean dishes as they hit the drying rack. As much as I find pleasure in this simple and routine task, I'm reminded of a time where simply doing the dishes led to a powerful revelation. It's wonderful to know that an omnipotent God can speak the loudest through the sounds of the smallest events of our lives.

Since I'm not much of a cook, I take great pride in washing the dishes for my wife. Yet, despite my best effort and intention, I committed what would be considered a cardinal sin by most women. One of my wife's favorite glasses inadvertently slipped from my soapy grasp and went crashing to the floor. *Crash!* The noise of the glass seemed like it could have awakened the whole house. The result was what looked like thousands of pieces of shattered glass spread across the kitchen floor. At the sight of the glass, I knew immediately that I was in big trouble and had a lot of explaining to do.

The intensity was kind of like the feeling in elementary school when you dropped your whole lunch tray in the cafeteria and all you heard was "Ohhhhhhhh"; like the whole school knew you dropped it. But as I peered down at my mistake, a thought entered my mind. I thought of how our lives are just as fragile as the glass I'd just dropped; and how like the tray in the school cafeteria, one slip and everything comes crashing down. That one moment in time, one car accident, one fall from a ladder, one random act of violence can change a person's life forever.

As I stared at the glass sparkling in the light on the kitchen floor, God began to reveal to me that the lives of so many people have been broken, marred, and damaged by one mistake, one bad decision, someone else's bad decision, or even one lapse in judgment. Like the shattering of the glass, I could see someone falling from the sky and there was no one with the reflexes to catch them before they hit the ground. The crash was deafening and the sound of the human spirit shattering because it was broken by an accidental slight of the hand; and when others looked to assess the damage, all they saw were broken pieces. All they saw were fragments of the former thing that was once so useful but is now so worthless. In fact, get out the broom and dustpan, and let's clean this mess up so that no one will even know it's broken! Then, let's put a selfie on social media and show everyone the clean floor and act as if nothing has ever happened.

So many people, regardless of whether they attend Church services, saint or sinner, Black or White, rich or poor, continue to find themselves picking up the pieces from real-life catastrophic events. The rise of homicides, suicides, school shootings, divorces, layoffs, and just dealing with life's ups and downs, is enough to break the human psyche while creating other mental and emotional challenges. As it is commonly said, "the struggle is real," and for many just to make it through to the next day is a miracle within itself.

When I dropped that glass and broke it, it was surely an accident. But can you imagine the terror of watching someone grab perfectly fine crystal glasses from a cabinet and begin to break them on purpose? It would seem as if that person had lost their mind and did not understand the value of the vessels they'd just destroyed. Not knowing the value of the items one has broken can cause a careless, nonchalant attitude, instead of a sincere apology. Yet, I am so glad that God isn't like man.

This same scenario can be used as an example to analyze our relationship with God. Our God is an intentional God, so it is no mistake when He performs the same task of breaking us. Oh yes, the ever-loving, mightiest in mercy, God of the everlasting, will with one sleight of hand, drop you into your destiny broken, to accomplish what He has set out to accomplish in your life. For surely, what God has determined to come to pass in your life, will be accomplished; no matter what! So, whatever gets broken in His hands, gets broken on purpose.

Understanding the will of God for your life must be a priority in order to see a bit clearer the journey God is taking you on. In contrast, having a clear vision that the painful times, the disappointing times, and the times that relationships, friendships, even careers were ripped from your grasp and thrown to the floor, were broken on purpose. Life is full of ups and downs, and the downs can sometimes cause us to question whether God knows exactly what He's doing. You're probably thinking, "God, can't you hear me, can't you see me, do you feel me? Where are you? Don't you see the broken pieces? Don't you see the shattered dreams?"

Nevertheless, I assure you the Lord knows exactly what He's doing and no one knows better about what's best for us than the Lord. Therefore, trusting God with your broken pieces and watching as He makes sense of the messes we've made, will help us to understand more clearly that God broke it on purpose. Walk with God through the pages of this book with me and see how He takes the broken lives of many in the Bible and piece by shattered piece, puts their lives back together again. No matter how damaged, how shattered, how broken you may feel, there's hope, there's healing, and there's help to put us all back together again. And as the smoke clears and your Heavenly Father comes into view, you'll realize He heard you all the time and see this was no mistake—He broke you on purpose.

1

Born Broken (Adam)

Before becoming a believer, I used to wonder why I was wired the way that I was. I knew my ways were off-kilter and I just could not seem to curve my destructive behavior. I struggled to tame the appetite that kept me outside of God's will and from becoming who God had desired me to be. My appetite kept me in the club on Fridays, Saturdays, and sometimes Sundays. My appetite kept me dissatisfied with just being with one female but would have one female coming in the front door, while one female was going out the back. My appetite kept me saying one drug, one drink was never enough. My appetite gave me a hunger and thirst for everything that was totally in opposition to the will of God. Yet, as a young man in my teens, God began to reveal to me that my struggle was the same struggle of the entire human race.

It can get crazy when you look in the mirror and know that you're better than where you are. It can be so hard knowing you can do better and wanting to do better but it seems like doing wrong is so much easier. When someone offends me, it is easier to hate them than it is to forgive them. If someone hurts me, it is much easier to seek revenge than to pray for them. When someone handles me unfairly, it is much easier to talk back, slap back, and "clap back". It's just in our nature to take the stance of, "If you do it to me, I'm going to do it to you back!"

In Psalms 51, God gave King David the same revelation. David said, "Behold, I was shapen in iniquity; and in sin did my mother conceive me." (Psalm 51:5). In other words, we were born to hit back. We were born to be self-centered. We were born to hear Jesus say, "Turn the other cheek," and reply to Jesus' request, "I'm not doing that, I'm not there yet!"

So I have to ask the questions, "You mean to tell me I was born broken? You mean to tell me I couldn't correct my condition?" You mean to tell me the Henessy, the fine women, the big money moves can't fix my broken condition? Can you imagine getting a brand new, seventy-five-inch, flat-screen Smart TV delivered to your home, after spending a grand, getting the stand or the mount, and you picked the perfect spot to entertain your girls, your guys, the click or the crew; only to discover that it had been broken or damaged before you took it out of the box? It was delivered to you broken. The screen was cracked before you even got a chance to watch your first show. You would probably experience feelings of outrage and immediately want to return it for a full refund or replacement. My hard-earned money was not designed to pay for broken products that don't do anything they are designed to do.

Well, God has that same issue with you and I. The only difference is that when he receives his package, which is you and I, even though he finds that we were born broken, he has no desire to send us back or get a replacement. Our all-wise God knows that the source of our brokenness is connected to our naughty nature.

This is the nature that keeps us doing the wrong thing and justifying our actions by claiming, "I'm doing the wrong thing but for the right reasons." Or, "I just can't help myself." Or, "This is just who I am." Before I received Christ as my Lord and Savior and became a believer, I tried to be good, I really did but it just didn't work. I tried to stop going from woman to woman but I just couldn't. I tried to stop going to the club but I just couldn't. I tried to be moral but my moral monitor was stuck on immorality. It was in my very nature to do wrong and I couldn't understand what side of the family I inherited this wild side from. Maybe my daddy's side, he could be as mean as they came. Or maybe my sweet mother's side of the family, who didn't mind giving you a piece of her mind either. No, this naughty nature came from the first man who left a universal defect in the nature of men. The first man who is the father of the human family was Adam. We can read about the events of Adam's life in the first five chapters of the Book of Genesis in the Bible.

When Adam sinned in the Garden of Eden, his DNA left a familiar strand that gave a common denominator to everyone who was born in Adam and after Adam, which was a sin nature. Adam's sin left us all with a nature that is opposed to the nature of God. The scripture says, "The carnal mind is enmity [the opposing force] against God: for it is not subject to the law of God, neither indeed can be" (Romans 8:7). Therefore, our nature is fueled by a broken covenant, a broken relationship, and a broken spirit from a broken man named Adam.

Being born broken is very difficult to overcome because putting the pieces back together again would take a miracle. I remember the time when I had an addiction that I just couldn't shake; because I couldn't break free of one addiction, other addictions developed. In my own strength, I tried to fix myself but I could not get my broken pieces back together again. I tried quitting cold turkey, but that didn't work. I tried self-help groups, but that didn't work, I tried everything I could think of but my addiction pulled me right back into my naughty nature.

People who struggle with co-dependencies are not always thinking rationally but God knows how to speak into the winds of our storms and light the way to deliverance. I can remember looking around me and saying, "I'm so tired of this. I'm tired of the drugs, I'm tired of the money, I'm tired of the clubs, I'm tired of the women, I'm tired of the death, the lifestyle of a thug." It all was getting old. It can be so frustrating when you're tired of the life you're living but you're in too deep. Have you ever been in too deep? Too deep into this relationship, to deep into this career, to deep into this mindset, to deep into this depression? There are some areas of our lives that only God can fix because we're in too deep. Please understand, no matter how low you've gone, or how deep of a hole you've dug for yourself; you can never be in so deep that God can't come and pull you out.

It was God's desire that Adam and his offspring experience a life of wholeness; however, the sins of our father, Adam, impacted the lives of his sons and daughters and life would no longer be the same. God did not create us broken but Adam got broken and everyone birthed from his kind (mankind) was born broken like Adam. Many of us fight daily to make it to our next moment without messing things up. We can get to a point in our lives where we are not just sick of other people's foolishness, but we are even sick of ourselves. Nevertheless, don't give up on yourself because God knows just how to fix your broken pieces. He knows we were broken from the beginning and it's all in the Master's plan to heal broken hearts, broken spirits, and broken minds.

The Bible says, "I can do all things through Christ which strengtheneth me" (Philippians 4:13). It's not our strength that fixes us but God's strength that He downloads into our hearts by His Holy Spirit. It's God's will that I am fixed. That's why God reveals Himself to us as a Potter and reveals that we are the clay while the Church is the wheel of the Potter that is used to mold and shape this broken vessel. This vessel was born broken and only the careful hands of the skillful Potter can put us back together again. Piece by shattered piece, He designs a new vessel.

Paul said, "If any man be in Christ, he is a new creature: old things are passed away; behold, all things are become new" (II Corinthians 5:17). Being born again begins the process of renewal from being born broken, to the Potter putting you back together again. "All things are become new" awakens my new level, my new mindset, my new breakthrough, my new outcome. Every day a new test and a new trial gauges our tolerance level to see if we will crack under pressure. So, God uses our day-to-day situations, both good and bad, to shape this broken vessel, and through His Holy Spirit our minds and hearts begin to be renewed.

Renewing, reshaping, and rewiring our thinking to think like God thinks, to see like God sees, and hear as God hears. You may feel you're so broken you can't be fixed. You've tried everything, and everything and *everyone* has failed. Jesus will not fail you. He knows how to ease you into your next level without breaking you more in the process. No, the road to healing is not easy, but your healing begins when you let go and let God. Our healing begins when we place ourselves in the Master Potter's hands because only He knows we were born broken but *Broken on Purpose* to become a new vessel in His hands. A new vessel operates under a totally different mindset.

The hand of God stretched deep into the filth I was in, where I thought I was in too deep, and lifted me up out of my dark place into His marvelous light (I Peter 2:9). When God began to put my pieces back together again I was approached by an old friend who was well acquainted with my old lifestyle. I was as broke as Job's turkey because I had just experienced a major setback in my life but my setback was God setting me up. The Lord will sometimes allow you to be put in situations that demand you to choose to be set back or set up. He approached me with an offer I could not refuse: a possible twenty grand and all it took was a handshake.

The old broken me would have shaken quicker than a California earthquake but the new me made a clear statement, "I'm not the man you once knew and the poison that people push will put me in prison." So I walked away from the Alan that Jesus crucified and walked into the Alan that Jesus resurrected. The new me showed up with a new mindset, a new desire, a new way to flex—now I flex with the strength of God. Will you show up when you're faced with the choice to walk away, so you can walk into the new you? When God puts your pieces back together again, you may not be perfect but the process is what keeps you on the wheel of the Potter. The more the Potter molds and shapes you, the more you understand that we all are broken but not by mistake; we are broken on purpose.

Application Exercise

Do you feel broken in any area of your life? What or who caused this brokenness to transpire?

Don't be afraid to "name your pain". Name it. Then, ask God to heal your broken pieces and accept the process.

_____

_____

_____

_____

_____

_____

_____

_____

_____

2

Broken Vessels

David revealed to us in Psalms 51:17, "The sacrifices of God are a broken spirit: a broken and a contrite heart, O God, thou wilt not despise." In that the Old Testament was written in the Hebrew language, it is good to see what David saw in his heart when he used the word *broken*. The Hebrew word for broken in this text is the word "shabar" (Strongs H7665). Shabar is defined as, "to burst, to break down, break off, break up or break in pieces, broken-hearted, to crush, destroy or hurt" (Strongs H7665). God already knows that we are born broken, broken off, broken in pieces as I acknowledged in the previous chapter. Born in our forefather Adam's broken nature, God already knows we are flawed with an inherent character that only He can correct.

It's so encouraging to know that despite how perfect and holy everyone else expects you to be, the Lord already knows that we're not perfect or holy without the help of His Holy Spirit; and even with the Holy Spirit, we still make mistakes and struggle with meeting God's standard of holiness. Yet, David said as he worshipped the Lord in the Psalm that the sacrifice of God is a broken heart. A heart that has experienced *shabar,* is a heart that has been broken down, broken off, and broken into pieces. This is the heart the Master is so willing to heal.

Life's experiences can destroy your heart and leave you broken. For instance, many adults struggle with childhood tragedies that left them shattered. Many share stories of the death of a parent, which left them feeling alone and abandoned, while others express feelings of insecurity and fear, or question their sexuality after being molested by an abuser. These individuals, and many with similar stories of pain, are screaming on the inside to have their broken hearts mended.

Maybe when you look into the mirror you scream from the inside and you feel that no one hears you. You remember the problem or the person that caused your breaking but no one wants to talk about the things you remember. God wants to heal our hearts from the things that keep us living as broken vessels. Some of us have no idea how broken we really are. In reality, you never know how broken a vessel is until you pour a liquid into it. Once the liquid fills the vessel, that's when you begin to see the liquid leaking through the cracks.

I'm reminded of a time I was trying to get used to the Southern heat. Being from Baltimore and relocating to South Carolina, I realized the heat of the noonday sun was relentless. I had just purchased a refreshing ice-cold drink from a fast-food restaurant. I paid for my drink and by habit sat it quickly and forcefully into the cup holder. What I did not know was that a staple had fallen into my cupholder. The staple was just sharp enough to pierce the bottom of the cup of my cool, refreshing drink. Without me realizing it, my drink began to leak into my cupholder. Man, was I hurt. Everything I purchased leaked out and made a mess.

Many saints and sinners cannot hold on to what God wants to pour into them because the anointing keeps leaking out through the cracks. Many are either afraid to deal with the secret issues that have created the cracks in their hearts, or they may be too arrogant to accept God's deliverance. Instead, they find contentment not battling their demons, but actually living with them. Petting your demons and accepting their unclean presence will not stop the leaking; it will only drip harder from a hidden place.

Imagine you have a leak in a pipe in the wall of your home and you hear the dripping but ignore the problem. It will eventually cause water damage and begin to show through the walls or the ceiling tiles. You can't hide the places that are leaking in your heart, in your spirit, or in your life. Eventually, the leaks will show through my mask and reveal stains in my marriage, my relationships, my career, my business, and my ministry. We must accept the broken places and believe God to heal, mend, and seal up our leaking hearts and spirits even in the secret and darkest parts of our lives.

As a youth, I was exposed to pornography very early by my peers. Many people would love to believe that pornography doesn't create life-long bondages, however, I remember the struggle it was for God to free me from a darkness I learned to love. St. John 3:19 shares with us, "...men loved darkness rather than light, because their deeds were evil." It was much easier to pet the thing the devil designed to kill me. When you seek to bring light to your dark places, it will be so much easier to see the cracks in your broken vessel.

Only the Lord can seal up our broken places and cause us to walk in wholeness. The Bible speaks in Haggai 1:6 of bags with holes that cannot hold water. The revelation here is that as long as we're broken, we won't be able to hold anything God has anointed us or empowered us to do. Relationships that are divinely connected will be forfeited because of the holes in the bag. The financial opportunities that can change the entire trajectory of our lives will be missed because we won't release financial blessings into the hands of others, nor believe God for a harvest; therefore there are holes in our bags.

When you refuse to let a disagreement go, your opportunity to forgive is hindered by bitterness and unforgiveness; this leaves holes in our bags. The things we neglect to share with others are sometimes because we have nothing left to give of ourselves. We look for it on the inside but sadly find what we need for that moment has leaked into the cupholders of our lives and we are empty. The devil knows this and uses the holes to keep us leaking.

When the enemy invades your home and you go to God for help and get no relief in your life, it's simply because you've got holes in your bag. These holes leave even the most faithful church member feeling empty and alone, but don't lose hope. When the Spirit of the Lord fills a believer with His presence, all the holes in our hearts, all the empty places, and all the leaks in our spirit are filled with God's love, grace, and mercy. Even beyond this, we then can access His divine healing power. The healing we need to recover and live life happy, whole, and blessed.

Please remember that healing is a process; some wounds run deep and some holes are larger than others. You may have been born broken but it still took time to live with being dropped and shattered again and again throughout life's journey. So as God begins to make you anew, understand that you are His work in progress. Your progress is a second by second, minute by minute, and day by day experience. The purpose of God is the path to your healing place. Purpose makes sense of the pain. It gives you understanding as to why there is pain and what it takes to get these hurts and holes mended in the Potter's hand.

So, fear not! It is your Father's good pleasure to have patience with you in this progressive process on your path to purpose. Broken vessels belong to God and are part of His divine purpose. His purpose connects the dots that reveal the progression of the cracks being healed. Progression comes with a move of God that slowly, but surely, seals up the cracks in our lives.

Application Exercise

The hardest part of the process is accepting the holes that continue to leak in your heart, mind, and spirit. People who are broken love to say, "There's nothing wrong with me!" But everyone around you sees the stained ceiling tile.

Write down what is leaking through into your life. For instance, think of the person, place, or thing that still makes you angry, sad, or nervous. Now ask God to heal up the hole and empower you to forgive the person, forsake the anger, attitude, aggravation, and embrace love, peace, and healing.

Broken Vessels

_____

_____

_____

_____

_____

_____

_____

_____

_____

3

Broken Just Like Us

As men and women in the 21st Century age, we contemplate whether anyone can feel our pain and the hurt of our struggle. We are prone to think we are the only ones dealing with our problems. Jesus does know everything we face as men and women, yet, we cannot limit our thinking that we have no real point of reference. We must understand that many are facing the same trials and tribulations that we are and God still gets the glory out of their situation and they're winning.

Broken people, whether broken by experience or broken on purpose by God, tend to feel isolated in their incident. However, God had patriarchs and matriarchs in the Bible who were just as broken as we are. God knew exactly who to add to the canon of the scriptures and He was looking for the people who never said they were perfect.

In Matthew 1:5, one young lady stood out among the genealogy of Jesus Christ. When the Jewish scholar read the names in chronological order they would know that Jesus was connected to a great Jewish lineage. Abraham, Issac, Jacob, and David were well-known among the Jewish culture with great esteem. These names brought great pride to the Jewish nation and their culture. These names are kind of like Albert Einstein for the European, or Martin Luther King, Jr. for the African American; Jesus was connected to greatness!

Yet, I'm sure it raised a Jewish eyebrow when in the family of Jesus Christ there was the mother of Boaz, named Rahab (Matthew 1:5). The Bible gives her a title in the Book of Joshua: they called her Rahab, the harlot. A harlot! Really, in the family of Jesus? Yes, a harlot was connected to the King of Kings and the Lord of Lords but God did this on purpose! Rahab was a resident of Jericho, the city God was about to overthrow in Joshua's day. She was the "town harlot" and her house was on the wall of the city to catch her suitors coming in and going out of the gate. Rahab was a woman of reputation or the scriptures would not have named her by her occupation.

Rahab got connected to the Jews because she helped the spies of Israel escape from the city of Jericho but made them promise to return the favor by saving her house when Israel returned to take the city (Joshua 2:13). Israel did return, took Jericho, and as promised, the spies saved Rahab and her house because of her kindness. According to Matthew 1:5, Rahab married a Jew named Salmon, the son of Nahshon, and together Salmon and Rahab had Boaz. Now her name is forever in the Word of God as the mother of Boaz. Rahab is forever a part of the bloodline of the Jewish Messiah Jesus Christ.

Rahab was a woman who knew what it felt like to operate in brokenness. From man to man, that only brought sexuality without intimacy, money without marriage, a service without sincerity. This woman knew what it felt like to be broken, but she knew what God looked like as well. When the opportunity to change her situation was presented, she stepped into her destiny. God broke her on purpose, so that other women and men who feel like they have gone so low that God could not lift them up, could have a point of reference for their own deliverance. The Lord inserted her name in the genealogy of Jesus Christ, to reveal to the Jewish people that God can choose the one men would reject and make a miracle out of their messy life.

People may name you by your occupation or your situation, but God will choose you in the middle of a mess and make you part of a miracle move of God. God chooses broken vessels so that when the cracks are mended and the pieces are repaired, then the repaired vessel gives glory to the God who is the mender of broken pieces. Maybe you can identify with Rahab because of a life of sexuality and sensuality, that created cracks in the heart of your vessel.

As a youth raised in one of the roughest projects in Baltimore, I was forced to grow up fast or possibly become a victim. Survival of the fittest was the order of the day. Making sure no one robbed me for my mother's food stamps when I went to the store to buy groceries, or knowing when I was about to get recruited into a drug clique. I had to make Big Boy Decisions in a twelve-year-old body. When it came to females, it was just natural to be nasty; to be Naughty By Nature. I was exposed to pornography, sexuality, and sensuality very early in life. This created cracks in my young vessel that leaked into my adulthood. The appetite that I had for women was the result of being exposed early to a perverted form of a natural, God-given pleasure. So the lifestyle of going from woman to woman was just an acceptable practice, in fact, the more girls you had, the better your reputation.

Someone else may have been exposed to sexuality through molestation and it created cracks in their vessel. Exposure to sexuality early in life can cause strong sexual bondages. Many Christians have issues with sexual sin but, like Rahab, one encounter with God can change everything. Accepting that you have a sexual struggle and beginning to operate in the power of the Holy Spirit to repent, resist, and renew your desires, like Rahab you will begin to walk in spiritual victory. Every struggle may not heal overnight, however, making Godly decisions, and asking God in prayer to heal the hurts that left cracks in your vessel, will begin the process of mending and making another or a new vessel.

Joseph was the younger of the sons of Jacob (Genesis 37:3). As the favorite of his father, he was raised in an environment full of sibling rivalry. Because Joseph was a dreamer with a vision of his future according to the will of God, envy in the hearts of his brothers made a day in the life of Joseph toxic. In the Book of Genesis, the account of Joseph's life tells the story of how his brothers sold him into slavery and broke his father's heart. Jealousy in a family can curse a generation.

Joseph was elevated in Egypt, the land of his captivity, and became a leader second to none but Pharaoh. The hand of God was in the middle of Joseph's struggle and even though his journey was painful, God had a plan and a purpose for his pain. When the famine affected the whole country and even his father's house, only Joseph had the plan to save the whole country. Joseph went through a great storm in Egypt. Yet Joseph said at the end of the story, "But as for you, ye thought evil against me; but God meant it unto good, to bring to pass, as it is this day, to save much people alive" (Genesis 50:20).

Have you experienced family issues that made you feel like you were sold into slavery? The difficult family life that Joseph experienced was all a part of God's perfect plan for his life. In fact, God did it on *purpose* to save many souls alive. Never despise your struggle. Just because your family isn't always supportive doesn't mean you're hated; it may mean that God separated you to save the ones who sold you. Many suffer in silence as they endure abuse in their own home. Jesus said that a prophet is not honored in his own city nor in his own home (Matthew 13:57). If your home has been hostile for you then remember, Joseph was the one God used not just to save his family but to save his nation, and eventually their preservation would birth their Messiah.

Families within the scriptures showed many dysfunctions that may have made the chiefest of sinners blush. One of the most infamous family breaks was the defiling of Tamar, the daughter of King David. In II Samuel 13:1 it says, "And it came to pass after this, that Absalom the son of David had a fair sister, whose name was Tamar; and Amnon the son of David loved her." In that she was the half-sister of Amnon, it was not forbidden for him to wed her as his wife but instead, Amnon chose to make himself stressed over her. Taking the advice of his friend, Amnon deceived Tamar, playing ill and demanding that he be nursed back to health only by her. As a result, Amnon made sexual advances toward his half-sister that she was willing to resolve lawfully by Amnon simply asking his father, the king, for her hand.

Yet, Amnon, being sick in love and full of lust raped his half-sister and defiled, shamed, and dismissed her. From this shattered situation, Amnon hated Tamar more than he loved her, which can be considered the common attitude of a man that does not respect a woman (II Sam 13). Tamar remained unmarried and her brother, Absalom, vowed to kill his half-brother Amnon.

This kind of dysfunction is very familiar in many families. Many have suffered molestation, rape, and assault at the hand of a family member. Suffering from this kind of abuse can damage the spirit of a man, woman, boy, or girl. This breaks relationships, it breaks trust in others, it even breaks trust in those who may not have anything to do with the crime. Also, surely this will break the spirit of the person who had to endure such an experience. Anything the devil uses to kill you spiritually, emotionally, or physically, God will use it to give you power, provision, and purpose. God commands us to obey those that have rule over us (Hebrews 13:17); by this, the law of the land prohibits that kind of abuse. Therefore, no one has to suffer in silence but God will reveal His will even through this kind of pain.

The scriptures speak of ordinary people, who did extraordinary things because of our supernatural God. Yet, these ordinary people suffered extraordinary tests and trials and some even paid with their lives. God left their testimonies as witnesses that if God got them through their rough times, He will also get us through our hard times. We have so many people in the Bible who made a difference in their families, their communities, and in their nations although they were broken just like us.

Even great prophets who prophesied to kings and nations were not exempt from having to face cracks in their armor. Elijah the Tishbite was found to be one of the greatest prophets of God in his day. He prophesied during the reign of Ahab, king of Israel, who was married to Jezebel. Jezebel was the daughter of King Ethbaal, king of the Zidonians, and they were worshippers of the false god Baal. King Ahab found himself so influenced by Jezebel's heathen ways, that the politically motivated marriage turned Ahab's heart from worshipping the true God of Israel. This reveals to every believer that no matter how strong you are, if you find yourself connected to the wrong people, other people can turn your heart from true worship.

Yet, whenever our hearts are not right toward God, He will always send a warning through the prophet to get us back on the right track. So God sent Elijah to prophesy to King Ahab and correct the errors of his ways, but Queen Jezebel despised Elijah and the God of Israel so much that she wanted nothing more than to destroy Elijah. In the eighteenth chapter of I Kings, Elijah was done talking and it was time to demonstrate the power of God. There are days God has you feeling like you're the king of the mountain. Your faith is strong and you feel so close to God that you can check His temperature. Elijah was feeling empowered and challenged the prophets of Baal and won the challenge of the God that answers by fire. Elijah had the prophets of Baal executed and the people received the blessing of rain in their drought.

Elijah was the hero, the champion, and I know he felt good about God showing how powerful He was in the life of Elijah. Yet, in the nineteenth chapter of I Kings, the very next chapter, King Ahab tells his wife Jezebel everything that Elijah has done. From Elijah humiliating the prophets of Baal, to their execution at Mount Carmel and the queen was enraged. I mean every hateful bone in her body was on fire with hate toward the Prophet Elijah. In verse 19:2 Jezebel makes it plain concerning her thoughts about this Elijah the Prophet. Jezebel declares, "So let the gods do to me, and more also, if I make not thy life as the life of one of them by tomorrow about this time."

Application Exercise

Remember, you are not alone in this fight. What the devil meant to break you, God can use to save you and others that may be *Broken Like Us*. Write a prayer to God letting Him know you understand you're not alone and that He connects you to people who are healed from similar hurt. This can help your healing process and that may help heal others.

_____

_____

_____

_____

_____

_____

_____

_____

_____

4

Blessed It, Broke It, and Gave It Away

In the Gospel according to St. Mark, in the sixth chapter, beginning at verse 34-44, the discourse is shared that after the profound words were taught by the Master Teacher, the people were hungry for natural food. They so desired to feed on food from the Kingdom that permeated from the mouth of Jesus, they had neglected to remember that they needed to nourish their natural bodies, which Jesus was well aware of. There is a place you can live in with God where the natural desires are dwarfed when compared to the things of the Spirit. Job said, "Neither have I gone back from the commandment of His lips; I have esteemed the words of His mouth more than my necessary food" (Job 23:12).

Sometimes God uses the broken seasons in our lives to cause our appetites to change. Where we crave His presence more than we crave a crowd, where we want to worship more than we want others to want us, where we weep for His Word more than we cry "victim" when we're criticized. Sometimes in your broken places you realize that God was all you were hungry and thirsty for all along. Whatever God allows to happen in our lives, He allows it with purpose in mind. God has pushed you to realize you are only satisfied when you sit at the feet of Jesus and are taught. The satisfaction is knowing that at the feet of Jesus is the life-changing word that heals a situation.

The text determines that Jesus had compassion on the people. When His disciples began to speak of the need to send them away that they may purchase food to eat, Jesus commanded His disciples to feed the people if they were hungry (Mark 6). Of course, His disciples considered the multitude of people and determined they lacked the resources financially. They considered how they lacked the ability to expand their thinking enough to bring chaos into collaboration. That is Jesus' speciality; to speak to you in the middle of your lack and bring forth abundance. He desires to speak into your chaos and bring forth peace. I thank God that Jesus doesn't need my permission to command me to solve a problem that I deem relevant but lack the resources and skills to solve. The problem has a purpose and that purpose is to glorify God. Therefore, the need is not that I solve the problem, but that I listen for the question and declare, "Lord thou knowest."

I don't have to lean to my own understanding, I can watch Him direct my path. Jesus, being fully aware that his comrades could not fix the problem, asked another problem solving question, "He saith unto them, 'How many loaves have ye?'" (Mark 6:38). Now, you may say, "All I have is broken pieces!" But God will take your broken pieces and feed a multitude.

In the Gospel according to St. John, chapter 6:9, a little boy had two fish and five loaves of bread; this could not feed a multitude. However, whatever you put in the hands of Jesus is a candidate for a miracle. In Mark 6:41, Jesus had everyone sit in companies, took control of the dilemma at hand, took a mess and made it a miracle. The disciples couldn't fix the problem of feeding 5,000 men, not including women and children. Jesus took the two fish and five loaves of bread. He blessed it, broke it, and gave it away. The little boy's lunch was divided from the hands of the Master and His disciples watched it multiply as they started giving, and giving, and giving.

You may feel that what you have to offer God has been beaten by life so badly it is insignificant, but if you put all your pain, sorrow, and disappointment into Jesus' hands, He'll use it to deliver the world. When God makes His choice regarding who He wants to use, it is not the normal viewpoint of man's wisdom because the wisdom of God makes man's wisdom foolishness (I Corinthians 2). He chose to use a little boy's lunch and never gave the child's name because all the glory had to go to God.

When you hand over your life to Jesus, He may break it but in the process of His breaking it, He will bless it. You may think, *Why in the world would God choose me? I just left the club, I just left the bar, I just left dancing on a pole, my marriage is broken, my addictions have broken me and in fact, I have just had a nervous breakdown!* Yet, He loves the broken. He said, "A broken and contrite heart He will not despise" (Psalm 51:17). God loves you and all your broken pieces. He knows that if He puts you back together and blesses your life, that only He will get the glory out of the life that man said was broken beyond repair.

In I Corinthians 1, the Apostle Paul makes it clear who is the Lord's choice. In man's eyes, it should be the strongest because we say, "Only the strong survive." In man's eyes, God should choose the biggest, because we say "the bigger, the better". In man's eyes, God should choose the smartest because we say "great minds think alike". In man's eyes, their choice is based on outward appearance, what looks good to them. But God's choice is the little boy or little girl standing in the background that nobody sees and no one wants to see.

> For you see your calling, brethren, that not many wise according to the flesh, not many mighty, not many noble, *are called.* But God has chosen the foolish things of the world to put to shame the wise, and God has chosen the weak things of the world to put to shame the things which are mighty; and the base things of the world and the things which are despised God has chosen, and the things which are not, to bring to nothing the things that are, that no flesh should glory in His presence.
>
> 1 Corinthians 1:26-29, NKJV

God wants all the glory for putting together your broken pieces because He chose you. He pulled you out of the shattered remnants and blessed you, and caused people to taste and see just how good He is. Your life is on display and God chose your life, as broken as you may feel it is, to bless you and give to a hungry and thirsty world. The word "blessed" is sometimes defined in its simplest terms as "happy" yet, in its original context, it is more accurately defined as "favor" or having obtained the favor of God (Smith's Bible Dictionary).

God has taken the one who is not supposed to have favor. He's taken the rejected, the despised, the weak, and even those some consider unwise, and made them His choice. You may feel like you're not God's choice, but even though you're at the back of the line, God wants what you have. Fish and bread may not seem like much to some but everything multiplies in the Master's hands. God's math doesn't match man's math. God's math says, you give it away and it will return to you one hundredfold. God's math says, when He divides it, everything you give multiplies.

Never be afraid when God gives you the opportunity to release your broken pieces into His hands because He will multiply what you give and your return will be immeasurable. God's math always adds to your life whether He's subtracting, multiplying, or dividing. All God wants is for those who are broken in spirit to release all the pain, disappointment, and discouragement to Him so that He can bless your life. God loves you and that love will never cease. That love will take what you deem small and bless it, break it, and give it away.

Application Exercise

What are the broken pieces of your life that you are willing to give to God? Write down ways God can use your broken pieces to bless others. Don't be afraid to share with others what God has blessed.

_____

_____

_____

Blessed It, Broke It, and Gave It Away

_____

_____

_____

_____

_____

_____

_____

_____

5

Broken Yokes: The Shift to My Purpose Path

The Bible gives us an account of the Prophet Elijah who performed great miracles and defeated great enemies of the Lord in the days of King Ahab. Yet even the successful ministry of the Prophet Elijah had to come to an end. His mantle had to be passed to a young man who would become a prophet of the Lord in his stead, and the Lord told Elijah just who it would be. In I Kings 19, the Lord spoke to Elijah concerning those He would put in place to preserve Israel. Elijah would appoint Hazael as King of Syria, and Jehu, the son of Nimshi, as king over Israel, and Elisha as the prophet of the Lord in Elijah's stead.

A "spiritual shift" was about to take place; not just in the dynasties of the monarchs of Israel and Judah, but in the prophetic utterance of the leader of the prophets of the Lord. This shift would take Elijah into the Kingdom of God and shift Elisha into his path to purpose. The scriptures tell us how the shift began in I Kings.

So he [Elijah] departed from there, and found Elisha the son of Shaphat, who was plowing with twelve yoke of oxen before him, and he was with the twelfth. Then Elijah passed by him and threw his mantle on him. And he left the oxen and ran after Elijah, and said, "Please let me kiss my father and my mother, and then I will follow you." And he said to him, "Go back again, for what have I done to you? So Elisha turned back from him, and took a yoke of oxen and slaughtered them and boiled their flesh, using the oxen's equipment, and gave it to the people, and they ate. Then he arose and followed Elijah, and became his servant.

I Kings 19:19-21, NKJV

Now, there are some powerful nuggets we must explore in the text so we don't take this discourse lightly. When God is about to shift you from broken to blessed, He sometimes finds you busy looking at the field you're plowing and speaking to yourself saying, "There's got to be more than this!" It's more than walking in circles to fulfill what mama sees in me. It's more than walking in circles to fulfill what daddy sees in me. You get a strange feeling that there's more to you than this. More than this job that's going nowhere, more than this relationship that's just so toxic, more than the ox, the plow, and the yoke. You feel like something awesome is about to happen but you can't put your finger on it.

Yet, you feel the shift in your spirit. You know you're in the right place, at the right time, for a mighty move of God. You feel God shifting you from one level of broken to a level of blessed, but the yoke is still on your neck and the plow is still in your hands. Sometimes you can feel like your life is full of broken things that have your neck in a yoke. Broken things that are forcing you to walk in circles but you're going nowhere.

Elisha was moving in the direction of his parents' vision for his life, which was not a bad thing, but God had called his name and pulled him out of his ordinary life and into an extraordinary shift. Though Elisha was plowing with a physical yoke of oxen, there was a spiritual yoke around his neck as well because the thing that you think you're in control of can actually be controlling you. Are you driving your life, or are you just being driven? Do you feel like you're the one in bondage; like you're the one with the yoke around your neck?

Now, the yoke was the tool used to bind the oxen to one another and force them to labor by pulling the plow that tilled the land. The yoke was a help to the farmer but bondage to the ox. The ox had no power to choose his "Purpose Path" because he was tied to those who served in similar situations as him. Often we want to be around people who carry the same yoke of bondages that we do. We enjoy the victim mentality and grow bitter when nothing changes in our lives. We continue walking in circles when we are being called to our Purpose Path. The mantle is to change your mentality so your thinking will go from bitter to better when you see things begin to shift.

Elisha knew the Prophet Elijah because of his fame in Israel and when Elijah cast his mantle on to Elisha's shoulders, Elisha sensed that a shift had taken place. Immediately his thinking changed and he understood his plowing days were over. Remember, the mantle is designed to change your mentality. The task of walking in circles was about to change and Elisha was ready for his next level in God. The text said, "Elisha left the oxen..." When you hear the call of God and you feel that shift in your heart, you are willing to leave everything and everyone behind because the mantle changes your mentality.

To go from broken to blessed, you can't be afraid when God starts shifting your thinking. Never feel you are deserting the people who can't go with you, you're just moving with the Mantle. If the guilt of leaving family and friends behind to fulfill the purpose of God overwhelms you, please refer to the book written by my wife, Dr. Shanta Chester, *It's Not Personal...It's Purposeful,* to help to free yourself from that yoke as well. The mantle represents the anointing of God that gives you the ability to complete the assignment you're about to receive.

Now, not everyone can go with you, but the shift pushes you out of the familiar and takes you into your place of purpose. In the text, Elisha made one request, let me go back and bid my family goodbye. Elijah basically said, go do whatever you got to do; it's your moment not mine. Whatever you do, please don't miss your moment. Mantles are not released because God doesn't have anything else to do; but the divine purpose of God says "It's your time, it's your season for a fresh anointing." Elisha went back and broke the yoke that he walked around in circles for years with, burned the yoke, and killed and cooked the oxen that pulled the yoke.

The thing that the devil is using to break you, God is giving you the power to break it. The thing you feel is driving you, God is giving you the power to set it ablaze. Elisha had no intention of missing his moment, he broke that yoke on purpose. The mantle was his moment to step into the next level in God. It's time for you to go higher and the yoke is the fence that separates you from your next level. Your yoke might be fear; a fear of heights, a fear of your lack of ability to complete the assignment. A fear of what he will say, she will say, or they will say can become a yoke that only you can break off your neck.

We cannot allow guilt to hinder us just because God said everybody can't go with you. It doesn't mean you just throw people away, but it does mean for the season you're about to step into that obedience to God supersedes emotional attachments. Also, your yoke could be a sin that has become bondage. You are free from sin by the blood of Jesus and God will give you the power to overcome temptation. Whatever your yoke is, are you going to allow it to stop your destiny, to detour your purpose?

Elisha had to choose to stay stuck or to move with the mantle; he decided to make a move. It's time for *you* to make a move! This shift that God is commanding of you is going to be life-changing. The yokes of your past and present must be broken, and must be broken on purpose. Elisha received a double portion of Elijah's anointing from God and performed twice as many miracles as Elijah did in his lifetime. God put Elisha on his Path to Purpose and his life was never the same again. God has a Purpose Path for you and the time is now to break that yoke, feed your family and friends, put on your mantle, and walk in your purpose.

God told Israel in Leviticus 26:13, "I am the Lord your God, which brought you forth out of the land of Egypt, that ye should not be their bondmen; and I have broken the bands of your yoke, and made you go upright." Elisha's yoke had him walking in circles and the yoke of Egypt on Israel had them walking bent over.

Your broken pieces will not define your destiny. What God has allowed, has shaped you into the vessel you are today, and every pressing moment has pushed you closer and closer to fulfilling your purpose in God. Do exactly what you were created to do for the Kingdom of God and living in victory because of it. That's what living in the purpose of God does, it fills the spaces in our minds that question why we went through what we went through, and where God was in the middle of our storm. Purpose gives me an understanding of what every shattered situation was for so that I might become a vessel of honor unto the Lord. You are a vessel of honor and God's breaking hasn't made you bitter, but better in so many ways. Just know that every breaking was intentional and your life is not a mistake because God loves you on purpose.

Application Exercise

Can you recall where God broke a yoke that had you walking in circles and you felt God shift your life or change your direction? Write what you remember in a few words about that yoke being broken and God changing your direction. Then write a short prayer thanking God for the shift.

_____

_____

_____

_____

_____

_____

Pastor Alan L. Chester

6

Broken Religion

Churches, Choices, and Coronavirus

Christianity continues to stand as one of the fastest-growing religions in the world, and the United States has been a benchmark for what the church is supposed to look like in comparison to the Kingdom. We are a nation of multimillion-dollar facilities that almost resemble the glory of Solomon's temple, and many will take stock in beautiful buildings to confirm our inside track with God. However, what God gave Solomon will never be duplicated again in history because it was designed for that dispensation and to awe those who will forever read of these powerful events in scripture.

I am not by any means criticizing the blessing of God on our great country, nor am I despising the prosperity we share as children of God to be a blessing to those at home and abroad; however, when we trust in things and stuff more than we trust in the God who gave us the things and the stuff, then we lose sight of the Kingdom and focus on the carnal. In the last few months our world, our nation, and our churches have been impacted by the spread of the coronavirus. At the time of publishing, there have been over 4 million confirmed cases in the United States. It is definitely the plague of the century. My opinion of this matter is not my focus here because opinions are like life's experiences–everyone has them. However, I speak only on matters as the *Lord* allows.

The conditions of the coronavirus have not just caused businesses, beaches, and government branches to close their doors, but churches are also empty buildings of quiet walls due to social distancing. As the pastor of a local church in South Carolina, as well as an employee of a large hospital, I had a choice to make. My choice was to close our church doors with respect to recommendations of social distancing, my first-hand experience of working in a healthcare facility, and most importantly, my love for my family and the saints of God, or continue allowing parishioners to congregate. I chose to close our doors and use live streaming to continue ministering the Word of God as many pastors did. Again, my effort in this chapter is not to judge pastors for their choices to remain open or close their doors, but to reveal that buildings of brick and mortar can be transformed into palaces for spiders without the worship, fellowship, and praises of the people of God.

I communed with God, my wife, Dr. Shanta Chester, and my brother in Christ, our Assistant Pastor Elder Daron Stewart to do what was best for the people of God that He allowed me to lead. Just before the Covid-19 pandemic began to really impact the United States, one of our ministers who serves under my leadership and operates in the prophetic shared a word from God after a rare experience near the end of our Sunday worship service. During the altar call our newly purchased fiberglass podium was broken and even though we were live streaming the breaking was not public but was isolated to those present for that service. God doesn't always expose your broken places for the world to see, however. He uses our private breaks to become fuel for compassion when others' broken pieces go public.

The minister asked permission to share a word from God in the prophetic, I handed her the microphone and silence broke out around the room. As she stood before a broken podium and a congregation that seemed genuinely concerned about broken pieces and everyone being okay, she turned to me and proclaimed, "Pastor, God said He has broken the traditions of men and religion in our church. God has given you a different vision for ministry and we will not be like every other church..."

The totality of the prophecy was for our ministry so I will not share all of it, however, my point is that God's view of religion is not the elegance of an edifice, the pomp of our prosperity, or the treasure of our traditions, but it is the breaking of the sounding brass and tinkling cymbals that we hold dear and a focus on the fortune of faith, the highlights of hope, and the luxury of love that makes the church a living organism and not just a religious organization.

The crisis of Covid-19 forced many churches to see that buildings are beautiful and we appreciate them, but building *people* is the purpose of the Kingdom. A full church building of worshippers is always a wonderful sight to see, yet a church full of broken, battered people are more of Jesus's concern as The Great Physician. God is so glorified by the building of the great people of God than the construction of multimillion-dollar facilities. For if the broken vessels that give their worship, devotion, and finances remain broken, then as leaders we have strained at a gnat and swallowed a camel (Matthew 23:24).

It is God's desire to see the people of God praying in the middle of a pandemic and not panicking. It is God's desire to see the people of God full of faith and not full of fear. It is God's desire that the people of God are a light in the season of lack, and that although the doors of our buildings have closed, the doors of the Church that Jesus built are open wide for whomsoever will. The coronavirus outbreak may have caused a crisis in our country but our country has Christ for our crisis, the cross for coronavirus, and the blood to cover every Believer who has been purchased with a price.

Oh yes, my friend, the spirit of religion had to be broken to repair the true religion our Bible teaches about. "Pure religion and undefiled before God and the Father is this, To visit the fatherless and widows in their affliction, and to keep himself unspotted from the world" (James 1:27, KJV). True religion is not authenticated in our buildings by flashing lights and powerful sermons but it is confirmed by our love for the lost and the lives of those, both saved and unsaved, who have fought to survive an unseen enemy.

This pandemic has pushed us from comfortable religion to transformable religion that is life-changing, effective, and impactful. We've learned to be patient while waiting in long lines to get soap and toilet paper that may or may not be on the shelves. We've learned to mass text and use social media to have church in our homes and still feel the Holy Ghost bring joy like a river. We've learned how to play Sorry!, Connect Four, and UNO with skill again and to do a happy dance when my son finally lets me score a touchdown on Madden; yes he let me! Our buildings never defined us because it is the Master Mender of Broken Pieces who gave His life to save a broken mankind, to heal a broken world, and to fix a broken religion on purpose.

Application Exercise

In the wake of the Covid-19 pandemic, we know that our God is still in control. Write a few words about how this season affected your life and then write a prayer for the healing of your city, your state, our great country, and our world that God created on purpose.

_____

_____

_____

_____

_____

_____

_____

_____

_____

References

King James Version Bible (1611)

Knowledge. (2013). Webster's All-In-One Dictionary & Thesaurus (5th ed.) Springfield, MA: Federal Street Press.,

Strongs, J., Kohlenberger, J.R., and Swanson, J.A. (2001). The Strongest Strong's Exhaustive Concordance of The Bible. Grand Rapids, Michigan: Zondervan

Smith, William, 1901, Smith's Bible Dictionary

About the Author

Pastor Alan L. Chester is the Pastor and Founder of Fresh Fire Ministries in West Columbia, South Carolina. He serves along with his wife, Dr. Shanta Chester, to inspire and strengthen the people of God to live their lives empowered by God's purpose. Pastor Chester has a Bachelor's of Science in Business, with a specialization in Health Care Management from Capella University. As an explosive preacher, husband, father, and health care worker, Pastor Chester continues to be a mentor and spiritual leader to many. He and his wife have a blended family of ten children.

CPSIA information can be obtained
at www.ICGtesting.com
Printed in the USA
BVHW091359141220
595676BV00014B/2195